50 Quick Ways to Help Your Students Think, Learn and Use Their Brains Brilliantly

By Mike Gershon

About the Author

Mike Gershon is a teacher, trainer and writer. He is the author of twenty books on teaching, learning and education, including a number of bestsellers, as well as the co-author of one other. Mike's online resources have been viewed and downloaded more than 2.5 million times by teachers in over 180 countries and territories. He is a regular contributor to the Times Educational Supplement and has created a series of electronic CPD guides for TES PRO. Find out more, get in touch and download free resources at www.mikegershon.com

Training and Consultancy

Mike is an expert trainer whose sessions have received acclaim from teachers across England. Recent bookings include:

- *Improving Literacy Levels in Every Classroom*, St Leonard's Academy, Sussex

- *Growth Mindsets, Effective Marking and Feedback* Ash Manor School, Aldershot

- *Effective Differentiation,* Tri-Borough Alternative Provision (TBAP), London

Mike also works as a consultant, advising on teaching and learning and creating bespoke materials for schools. Recent work includes:

- *Developing and Facilitating Independent Learning,* Chipping Norton School, Oxfordshire

- *Differentiation In-Service Training,* Charles Darwin School, Kent

If you would like speak to Mike about the services he can offer your school, please get in touch by email: mike@mikegershon.com

Other Works from the Same Authors

Available to buy now on Amazon:

How to use Differentiation in the Classroom: The Complete Guide

How to use Assessment for Learning in the Classroom: The Complete Guide

How to use Questioning in the Classroom: The Complete Guide

How to use Discussion in the Classroom: The Complete Guide

How to Teach EAL Students in the Classroom: The Complete Guide

More Secondary Starters and Plenaries

Secondary Starters and Plenaries: History

Teach Now! History: Becoming a Great History Teacher

The Growth Mindset Pocketbook (with Professor Barry Hymer)

How to be Outstanding in the Classroom

Also available to buy now on Amazon, the entire 'Quick 50' Series:

50 Quick and Brilliant Teaching Ideas

50 Quick and Brilliant Teaching Techniques

50 Quick and Easy Lesson Activities

50 Quick Ways to Help Your Students Secure A and B Grades at GCSE

50 Quick Ways to Help Your Students Think, Learn, and Use Their Brains Brilliantly

50 Quick Ways to Motivate and Engage Your Students

50 Quick Ways to Outstanding Teaching

50 Quick Ways to Perfect Behaviour Management

50 Quick and Brilliant Teaching Games

50 Quick and Easy Ways to Outstanding Group Work

50 Quick and Easy Ways to Prepare for Ofsted

50 Quick and Easy Ways Leaders can Prepare for Ofsted

About the Series

The 'Quick 50' series was born out of a desire to provide teachers with practical, tried and tested ideas, activities, strategies and techniques which would help them to teach brilliant lessons, raise achievement and engage and inspire their students.

Every title in the series distils great teaching wisdom into fifty bite-sized chunks. These are easy to digest and easy to apply – perfect for the busy teacher who wants to develop their practice and support their students.

Acknowledgements

As ever I must thank all the fantastic colleagues and students I have worked with over the years, first while training at the Institute of Education, Central Foundation Girls' School and Nower Hill High School and subsequently while working at Pimlico Academy and King Edward VI School in Bury St Edmunds.

Thanks also to Alison and Andrew Metcalfe for a great place to write and finally to Gordon at KallKwik for help with the covers.

Table of Contents

What's being said? What's being thought?

Who might I be?

What might happen next?

Strange Noises

Connect the Video

Reflection

Dominoes

Concept Maps

Draw Your Brain

Shape and Colour

Odd One Out

Recipe Time

What would win and why?

What's the story?

Improvements

Silent Conversation

Do It Yourself

That Packs a Jolt!

Best Question

Question Pass It On

If this is the answer, what is the question?

Question Yourself

Movement Breaks

Introduction

Welcome to '50 Quick Ways to Help Your Students Think, Learn and Use Their Brains Brilliantly.'

This book is packed full of exciting, creative ideas you can use in your classroom to support, inspire and engage your students.

The emphasis throughout is highly practical, presenting you with fantastic strategies you can employ to help your pupils think, learn and use their brains brilliantly.

All the entries can be used across the curriculum and with different age groups. You can also adapt them to suit your teaching style and the needs of the particular students you teach.

So, from one teacher to another, read on, enjoy and get those brains working!

Why? Cards

01 Why, oh why, oh why?

Why this and why that?

Why, why, why, why, why?

Why not make a set of cards for each table in your classroom containing a set of 'Why?' questions on them?

Why not ask students to pull cards out of the decks at random and use them to quiz each other (or themselves)?

Why not have a set of cards at the front of the room and pull 'Why?' questions out yourself to put to the whole class?

Why not use the 'Why?' cards when you are questioning students?

Why not encourage pupils to walk around the room using the 'Why' cards to question each other?

Why not?

Thought Bubbles

02 What is going on inside our heads? What is going on inside other people's heads? If it's our own heads, usually the best thing to do is to have a think and maybe do a bit of talking or some writing. If it's other people's heads, we need to get them to communicate with us in some way.

Here are two examples of how you can use thought bubbles to help pupils think about what is inside their own heads as well as what is inside other people's heads:

- Display an image on the board containing one or more people. Have a thought bubble coming off the top of one of the people's heads and ask students to discuss in pairs what they might be thinking and why.

- Ask students to draw a thought bubble and then to fill it in with everything they are thinking about the lesson (and you could follow up by asking them to discuss their filled-in thought bubbles with a partner).

Finger Thoughts

03 Sometimes when you ask a question to your class, or to individual students, they can look back at you non-plussed, uncertain or confused. They don't know what to think!

Help them out by using this method.

When you pose a question, ask students to think of five thoughts, one for each of the fingers on their hand (including the thumb, which I know some will say is not a finger, but let's just go with it here!).

Indicate that the first finger is for the simplest idea and that each subsequent finger should have an increasingly complex thought attached to it.

If you have pupils working in pairs, ask them to discuss their ideas and to agree on a set of finger thoughts between them, ready to share with you or with the whole class.

Top Three

04 Another way to help students use their brains effectively is to ask them for their top threes. This specifies the response you would like. Many students find this an easier way in which to think than if they are just asked for a general answer.

Here are some examples:

- Is this a good argument? Talk to your partner and come up with your top three reasons why it isn't.

- How could we test to see if this is true? Come up with your top three methods.

- What do you think about the question? Talk to your partner and decide what your top three thoughts are.

Another Brain

05 Sometimes we can find a lot out about a subject by imagining we were inside someone else's brain. I don't mean literally! That would be gross. But metaphorically it is like we are putting on someone else's thinking spectacles and having a look to see what they see.

Here are three ways you might help students to think through someone else's brain:

- Present pupils with a character (this could be someone specific or it could be a generic figure) and ask them to discuss with their partner how this person might view the topic of study.

- Present a question connected to the topic alongside three different characters. Ask students to come up with a possible answer each person might give.

- Give students a character to role-play and ask them to think like that person for the entire lesson.

Tell 3 People

06 Creating opportunities for effective, critical discussion is really important if we want students to use their brains brilliantly. When we talk about ideas analytically we move our thinking forwards, particularly if we are accessing viewpoints and perspectives with which we are not familiar.

A really simple, really effective technique which allows you to bring critical discussion into your lessons at nearly any point works as follows:

Set students a task to complete individually. This could be answering a question, noting down first thoughts on a topic or responding to a statement. Then, ask them to stand up, take their notes with them and tell three other people in the room about their ideas (sparking up a discussion on each occasion).

The What If...? Box

07 What if the world was a cube?

What if tomorrow the rivers turned to ice-cream?

What if the internet had been invented fifty years earlier?

'What if...?' questions help pupils to think creatively. They encourage speculation, imagination and reasoning (in order to explain why what you think might actually be a good answer).

You can come up with your own 'What if...?' questions, ask students to develop their own, or make use of my free resource, The What If...? Box available at www.mikegershon.com.

Tables

08 Sometimes, using your brain brilliantly means finding ways to take information out of it and recording this in a way that is simple and easy-to-use. One approach involves tables.

Tables help us break down information. They allow let us re-present it to ourselves in a way which is logical, categorised and clear.

Students aren't always aware of how useful tables can be. To help them appreciate their utility, include sections in your lessons where pupils tabulate information.

If anything was possible...

09 Assumptions are the limits of our world. It's like the old story about the elephant that was chained to a pole from the moment he was born. When they took the chain off, he never moved more than a chain's length away from the pole.

The reverse of this kind of mindset involves imagining that anything might be possible. If you can get your students thinking this way, who knows what great ideas they will come up with?

You can help your pupils to think that anything is possible by using creative activities in your lessons, asking open-ended questions, encouraging exploration of ideas and new possibilities and by using the word 'might' within your questions (compare 'What is the answer?' with 'What might the answer be?').

Words in Their Mouth

10 Thinking about other people's thoughts is a big part of thinking brilliantly. Developing an understanding of the possible ideas and views others might hold allows us to see a wider range of perspectives in our own minds. This, in turn, helps us to be more creative, more imaginative and more critical.

A good way to get students started down this path involves displaying an image on the board containing one or more people connected to the topic (alternatively, give this to pupils as a hand-out). Include speech bubbles coming from the people's mouths and ask students to imagine what they might be saying and why.

Develop the activity by having pupils compare their answers with one another.

Three New Things

11 Getting students to think and learn is the number one aim for any teacher. What we maybe don't always think about is whether we want that thinking and learning to stop at the school gates. Most of us, when we reflect on the issue, would say that no, we don't. In fact, we want pupils to be thinking and learning throughout their lives, whether they're at school, at home or somewhere else.

Socrates summed this up when he said, 'The unexamined life is not worth living.' Perhaps he was going a bit far for what we want, but the sentiment still rings true.

Encourage your students to be mindful of thinking and learning outside of school by challenging them to pick out three new things they come across during the course of the week, during the time they are not in school. Ask them to share these with each other at the start of your next lesson.

Solve a Problem

12 Pupils are solving problems all the time in their lives. They might be working out how to rearrange their bedroom, planning how to ask for more pocket money or building a castle in their back garden.

We can tap into this everyday aspect of students' lives by asking them to write about a problem they solved. They can then go on to imagine how they might apply the same skills to a problem connected to the topic of study.

You can do this with pupils at the beginning of a lesson or just prior to an activity which includes problem-solving.

Create a Problem

13 Here's another great idea connected to problem solving which will really get your students using their brains.

When pupils are fairly familiar with a topic, ask them to move into pairs and to create a problem connected to the topic in question. Then, invite them to work with their partner to try to solve the problem.

You can help students develop problems by giving them categories to think about or by providing them with sample problems to use as models.

As an alternative, you might ask pairs to develop problems for other pairs to try to solve.

Enterprising

14 In life many successful people are enterprising. They use their brains to solve problems, find solutions, identify ways to make money and predict new trends.

You can help your pupils to think in this way. Here are four examples of how:

- Include lots of problem-solving in your lessons. You can turn anything into a problem by only giving students some of the information and asking them to work out the rest.

- Ask pupils to come up with three or four different solutions for the problems you set them. Then, encourage them to test, rank or assess these to see which is best.

- When studying a topic, set students the challenge of working out ways in which a business could make money from the ideas or information connected to it.

- Ask pupils to invent new products based on the things you study. Encourage them to think about how they would market these so that they caught on.

Life Improver

15 Similar to being enterprising is thinking about how you can make life better for people – be that through a new product, a solution to a problem or the discovery of an answer to a major question.

You can help your pupils to think in this life-improving way by asking them to do any of the following for homework:

- Work out one way in which you could improve the lives of the people in your street. Bring in your ideas and be ready to present them to the rest of the class.

- Invent a solution to a problem connected to the topic which is troubling people in the world at the moment. (You might need to present some example problems to get the ball rolling).

- Find a way to make life better for everyone living in our country. What would you do? How would it change people's lives for the better?

If this is the solution, what was the problem?

16 This one is all about reverse-engineering. Instead of giving pupils a problem to solve, you give them the solution and ask them to work out what the problem was in the first place.

This varies in terms of difficulty depending on what you present to them. Some solutions are obviously connected to certain problems whereas in other cases the identification of a link is rather trickier.

Play around with different solutions and problems relevant to your subject; see which cause your students to use their brains the best.

Set Them Up and Knock Them Down

17 Here is another variation on problem-solving. It will help you to help your students think, learn and use their brains brilliantly.

Present your class with a problem connected to what you are studying. Next, show them five possible solutions to the problem. Ask students to work in pairs. They should discuss each of these solutions in turn before ranking them overall from most to least likely to work. Indicate that pupils should be ready to justify their answers (either to you or to their peers).

If you have time, you can get your students to explore and test the various solutions. This will then help them to reflect on the quality of the ranking order they first developed.

Make a Prediction

18 Because predicting things requires a lot of learning and a lot of thinking. You have to know about what has gone before, assess what might happen next, estimate the various probabilities connected to these possibilities and then, finally, be ready to justify your decision (and analyse why you were wrong if something else happens instead).

A really easy way you to build prediction into your lessons involves stopping the whole class at certain points and asking them to predict what they think will happen next, either in terms of the learning as a whole or in relation to a specific thing you are learning about.

Don't forget to ask students to justify the predictions they make (and to reflect on them afterwards).

Different Feelings

19 Display a statement on the board such as: "All taxes will be scrapped tomorrow and replaced by voluntary philanthropy."

Next, present students with three different people connected to the statement and ask them to think about how each one would respond and why. In this example we might say:

How might a millionaire feel about this?

What about a person on an average income?

And what about someone who is unemployed?

Pupils will have to use their brains to really try to empathise with the different positions the various people occupy. This will help them to think in different directions about the topic.

The Same, But Different

20 The better we use our brains, the more we pick up on the subtle differences between things – as well as those similarities we might miss at first glance.

This process is the development of nuance; an ability to see the world in shades of grey rather than as a canvas of black and white.

As an example, consider something with which you are closely familiar. Think about the way in which you view and understand that thing now compared to your first encounters.

Help students to develop nuance by using lots of compare and contrast activities in which they analyse the similarities and differences between various disparate items.

What's being said? What's being thought?

21 This is a variation of entries 5 and 10.

Find an interesting picture connected to the topic of study and which involves at least two people. Print this out so that it is in the middle of a piece of paper with plenty of white space around it.

Ask pupils to get into pairs. Hand a copy to each pair in the class and ask them to imagine what the people in the image are saying or thinking. They can write their ideas in the space around the image (and, if they have different coloured pens, they can use these to distinguish the different ideas they have).

When sufficient time has passed, invite pairs to team up into fours. They should then share and compare their answers.

Who might I be?

22 You can encourage speculation, prediction, reasoning and imaginative thinking with this activity. It is especially good when used at the beginning of a lesson.

Don't tell students what the topic is but do present them with an image of someone connected to it. Ask them the question: Who might this be?

Point out little bits of the picture that offer clues and encourage pupils to use these as a starting point for their reasoning. You might also like to reveal some further clues or offer some cryptic hints as time passes to help students in their quest for identification.

What might happen next?

23 This is another activity which works well at the start of a lesson and which, again, combines prediction, speculation, imagination and reasoning.

Either present your class with an image or play them a video and then pause it at a crucial moment. Whichever option you go for, ask your students to discuss with a partner what they think might happen next and why they think this.

The focus here is less on getting the correct answer and more on using evidence and reasoning to justify the suggestions put forward.

Strange Noises

24 This entry is a bit wacky but, stay with me, wacky can be good!

Play your students some strange noises (at least, they will be strange to begin with) connected to the topic of study (which you can reveal in advance or not mention) and ask them to discuss with their partner what they think these might be.

Repeat the noises once pupils have started discussing so that they can apply their ideas in real-time.

Ask different pairs to share their thoughts and to explain the reasoning behind their suggestions. Then, reveal the cause of the noise and talk to your class about its relevance.

Here's one great sounds site to get you started: http://sounds.bl.uk/

Connect the Video

25 This one is on a similar theme to our last entry, Strange Noises. Instead of using a noise as stimulus material for sparking off a critical and creative discussion, use a video. Show it to students and ask them how they might connect it to the learning from last lesson, the topic you are studying or an idea or piece of information you flag up.

What with YouTube's availability and ease-of-use, finding interesting or relevant videos has never been simpler: www.youtube.com.

Reflection

26 Reflection is an absolutely vital part of thinking effectively and using your brain brilliantly. Reflecting helps us to become aware of the thought processes we have used, as well as the strengths and limitations we have uncovered during our learning.

Regular reflection will help your pupils to develop metacognitive skills. That is, they will get better and better at thinking about thinking. This, in turn, will mean they are in a stronger position to use their brains brilliantly.

Have a look at my free resource, Plenaries on a Plate, for 168 reflection-style questions and activities, all ready-to-use and stored in one place.

Dominoes

27 This is a really fun activity you can do with your whole class. It sees them having to think really carefully about all sorts of ideas connected to the topic you are teaching.

Create a set of dominoes cards, enough so that there is one for every pupil. Each domino should have a question on one side and an answer on the other. Now, here's the twist (have you guessed it already?). The dominoes are handed out to students and the whole class then have to arrange themselves in order, so that every corresponding question and answer are matched up.

Lots of thinking, talking and brilliant use of brains will swiftly ensue!

Concept Maps

28 Concept maps are ways of visualising the connections we have in our minds. Ask students to take a key concept connected to the topic you are studying and to create a map with this at the centre. Coming off in all directions will be concepts, people, events, case studies, examples and so on.

You can ask students to annotate and illustrate their concept maps, to compare them with each other and to add to them or rewrite them as time goes on.

The whole process helps pupils think carefully and critically about the big ideas they are studying.

Draw Your Brain

29 Here's a nice short and simple one to use at the end of lessons. Ask students to draw their brains and to fill these outlines with everything they have learnt during the session (or unit).

Have a few outlines of brains to hand in case anyone is struggling to get their image right. You can find plenty of free ones ready for printing by image searching for 'Brain Template' on Google.

Shape and Colour

30 This is an activity that will stretch the brains of every student in your class. Near the end of the lesson, ask pupils to use only shape and colour to create an image of their learning. They should then share this with their partner, who has to try to guess what the learning is.

As you can see, this activity can be transferred to nearly any part of the lesson. You could ask students to represent an idea using only shape and colour, an event or even a process. Whatever you set them, make sure they know they will have to explain and justify the decisions they make!

Odd One Out

31 Display a collection of words or phrases on the board and ask students to work out which is the odd one out and why. The words or phrases should be connected to the topic you are studying and the activity is a good way in which to introduce a lesson.

You can invite pupils to identify an odd one out on their own or in discussion with their partner.

It may be the case that there is a clear odd one out, however, there doesn't need to be! The real benefit of this activity comes from the reasoning you are encouraging. Therefore, as long as students are putting forward and defending ideas, they will be using their brains brilliantly.

As a development, why not use pictures instead of words?

Recipe Time

32 Ask your students to write a recipe outlining the learning they have done during the course of the lesson. Indicate that they should begin by developing an ingredients list. Then, they should come up with a set of instructions akin to the method of making you see in traditional recipes.

This activity is effective at the end of lessons (or right at the end of a unit of work) as it causes pupils to look back at everything they have done, reinforcing the learning in their minds.

What would win and why?

33 Here's a fun activity you can use at nearly any point in your lesson.

Introduce students to two different things connected to the topic and ask them: 'What would win and why?'

Obviously this works better when the two things in question are people, groups or creatures. However, you can adapt it to work with ideas and inanimate objects as well – just be a little creative! It will certainly get your students thinking carefully and using their brains brilliantly.

What's the story?

34 Narrative is a central part of human life. We tell stories all the time and, in fact, some psychologists and philosophers believe that story-telling is a fundamental part of what it means to be human.

Tap into narrative in your lessons by presenting students with a series of connected images and asking them: What's the story?

Encourage paired discussion before asking various pupils around the room to share and explain their ideas.

It might be that you use this activity as a way into a particular topic or idea, with the story acting as a bridge which contextualises an abstract idea or unusual concept.

Improvements

35 How could X be improved?

Why would your changes be an improvement?

Who would they benefit?

How long would they last?

This is a simple activity you can use to get your students thinking critically and imaginatively about an idea, event, process or piece of information. You could even develop it by having pupils try to convince the rest of the group that their improvement is better than anybody else's.

Silent Conversation

36 Divide the class into groups of three. Give each group a large sheet of paper. Introduce a statement or question connected to the topic which you want pupils to discuss. Explain that this will be a silent conversation!

Students should take it in turns to write their thoughts and ideas down on their piece of paper. They should aim to create a continuous conversation. Each new point should flow from the previous one written down.

Develop the activity by having groups swap their pieces of paper before analysing and evaluating what their peers have written.

Do It Yourself

37 DIY, or do it yourself, is traditionally known to refer to the completion of tasks and improvements around the home. Here, we take the concept and turn it around to help pupils think, learn and use their brains brilliantly.

Wherever possible, look for opportunities to pass work on to students. By this I mean, avoid doing it yourself! For example, a pupil might ask you a question and your natural reaction would be to answer and help them. However, maybe it would be better to say: "Well what do you think?" or, "How could you try to answer that?"

The general point is that you should aim to make your students independent.

That way they will be thinking more, learning more and using their brains more.

That Packs a Jolt!

38 Some questions just make you sit up and think:

What is the nature of the universe?

Where does hope come from?

Can you prove that free will exists?

Asking questions like these – big questions which cut to the core – can jolt pupils out of a slumber, causing them to think big, exciting thoughts about your subject and the topics you are studying.

Best Question

39 Here's another nice technique based on questioning. Give every pupil in your class a slip of paper and ask them to come up with the very best question they possibly can. These could either be linked to the topic of study or they could be completely random.

Stress to your pupils that a really good question just won't cut it. These have to be the **best** questions possible!

When every student has written a question, collect them all in and then choose ones at random to read out to the class. These should stimulate some great discussions in which serious brain work takes place.

Question Pass It On

40 This activity is slightly more complex than some of the others but is good fun, with the potential to get somewhat anarchic.

Have your students sit in rows. Give the person at the end of the row a question. Explain that they have to pass this on; the questions are sent along the rows until they reach the end.

Then, pupils have to send back their answers. The catch is that every student must send an answer back to the start of the row but that every answer must be different. This means each pupil in turn has to remember and repeat all the previous answers as well as come up with one of their own.

Finally, if you want to make the activity really manic, set it up as a race between rows.

If this is the answer, what is the question?

41 A simple way to get students thinking deeply and using their brains.

Present them with a word, sentence, paragraph or phrase and then ask:

If this is the answer, what is the question?

Question Yourself

42 If you want your pupils to learn, think and use their brains brilliantly, ask them to question the work they produce. Provide a list of questions students can use. It might be that you ask them to go through every question or, alternatively, to pick out two or three on which to focus. Here are some sample questions:

- What would make this work better?

- Where have I put in high levels of effort and what are the results?

- How did I solve problems?

- If someone else had done this work, how might they have done things differently?

- Why might this not be the very best I can do? How could I change things next time?

Movement Breaks

43 Sometimes, particularly in longer lessons, students can get a bit sleepy, or they can lose some focus. If either of these things happens it means that pupils are no longer thinking, learning or using their brains to the degree we want.

Mix things up by using a movement break. This sees you and the whole class moving around a bit so as to break up the lesson, get the blood pumping and replenish the energy levels in the room.

You can find a collection of fun movement breaks in my free resource, available at www.mikegershon.com.

Thinking Tools

44 These are anything students can use to help them think more clearly. Examples include:

- Lists

- Scrap paper

- Tables

- Charts

- Dictionaries

Encourage pupils to use a variety of thinking tools when they are stuck. This will help them to use their brains better. It will also give them problem-solving strategies which they can apply repeatedly in future lessons (and beyond).

Mr Wrong

45 Give students the wrong answer and ask them to explain why it is wrong. For example:

- 3+8 = 12

- Potassium is an unreactive element

- Paragraphs should not be used in prose writing.

Develop the activity by having students come up with their own wrong answers which they then ask their peers to explain.

Word Limits

46 If you have a word limit then you have to think more carefully about what you are trying to say. This is as true of speech as it is of writing. You can set word limits for your pupils in all sorts of tasks. For example:

- When answering a question verbally

- When answering a question in writing

- When producing a poster or presentation

- When writing a story

- When in discussion (each student can only say a certain number of words before they lose their turn to speak)

The Same, But Less

47 Ask students to rewrite their work or to re-speak something they have said only, this time, using fewer words to convey the same meaning. The task is a tough one and pupils will have to think really carefully in order to be successful.

Tag It

48 Here's a super end of lesson activity you can use; one which will most likely enthuse and energise your students.

Display some graffiti tags on the board. You can find examples as part of a how-to guide at www.wikihow.com/graffiti-tag.

Next, ask your pupils to create a graffiti tag which symbolises the learning they have done in the lesson. Indicate that they will have to explain and justify their choices and design to their peers.

Conclude by having students show and discuss their work with each other.

No Words

49 Ask your pupils to explain an idea connected to the topic without using any words. This is usually really tough and will definitely get them using their brains brilliantly!

If you want to provide some assistance, give students a list of ways in which they can communicate without words:

- Through symbols

- Through images

- Through mime

- Through models

- Through diagrams

- Through cartoons

- Through gestures

I'm Joking

50 And so we finish our tour of 50 quick ways to help your students think, learn and use their brains brilliantly by invoking the gods of comedy and saying, why not ask your pupils to construct jokes connected to the topic you are studying?

Making a good joke is a tricky business. It requires careful thought, testing of alternatives, awareness of the likely responses of others and clear knowledge of the topic in question.

Try it out – ask your students to come up with jokes and then ask them to try these out on each other. The results may even raise a smile or two!

A Brief Request

If you have found this book useful I would be delighted if you could leave a review on Amazon to let others know.

If you have any thoughts or comments, or if you have an idea for a new book in the series you would like me to write, please don't hesitate to get in touch at mike@mikegershon.com.

Finally, don't forget that you can download all my teaching and learning resources for **FREE** at www.mikegershon.com.

13015369R00037

Printed in Great Britain
by Amazon.co.uk, Ltd.,
Marston Gate.